Gregor Mendel's Genetic Theory

Understanding and Applying Concepts of Probabilty

Bonnie Coulter Leech

PowerMath™

The Rosen Publishing Group's
PowerKids Press™
New York

Published in 2007 by The Rosen Publishing Group, Inc.
29 East 21st Street, New York, NY 10010

Book Design: Haley Wilson

Photo Credits: Cover (Mendel), pp. 5, 29 © Bettmann/Corbis; cover (wrinkled peas), p. 23 (wrinkled peas)
© Layne Kennedy/Corbis; p. 7 © Brownie Harris/Corbis; pp. 9, 10, 12, 13, 15 by Maura McConnell;
p. 11 © SuperStock; pp. 16, 17, 21, 27 © PhotoDisc; p. 23 (round peas) © Brendan Regan/Corbis;
p. 25 © Terry W. Eggers/Corbis.

Library of Congress Cataloging-in-Publication Data

Leech, Bonnie Coulter.
  Gregor Mendel's genetic theory : understanding and applying concepts of probability / Bonnie Coulter Leech
      p. cm. — (Math for the real world)
  Includes index.
  ISBN 1-4042-3355-5 (lib. bdg.)
  ISBN 1-4042-6063-3 (pbk.)
  6-pack ISBN 1-4042-6064-1
  1. Genetics—Juvenile literature. 2. Mendel, Gregor, 1822–1884—Juvenile literature. 3. Mendel's law—
Juvenile literature. 4. Probabilities—Juvenile literature. I. Title. II. Series.

  QH437.5.L44 2006
  576.5'2—dc22

                          2005012656

Manufactured in the United States of America

Contents

Who Was Gregor Mendel? 4

Working with Probability 6

Theoretical and Experimental Probability 14

Combinations 18

Genetics and Probability 20

The Father of Modern Genetics 30

Glossary 31

Index 32

Who Was Gregor Mendel?

Gregor Johann Mendel was born on July 20 or 22, 1822, in Heizendorf, Austria (now Hyncice, Czech Republic). Mendel's parents were peasant farmers. Living on a farm helped Mendel develop a love of nature and an early curiosity for learning. As a young man, Mendel attended the Olmutz Philosophical Institute but did not have enough money to finish school. In 1843, Mendel became an Augustinian monk in Brunn, Austria (now Brno, Czech Republic). There he continued his education without financial worries.

Mendel was not happy as a monk. He left the monastery and enrolled in the University of Vienna, where he studied physics, mathematics, and natural history. After 2 years, Mendel returned to the monastery at Brunn and became a teacher of science in the high school.

Mendel is best known for his experiments with **genetic** development and **inheritance**. During his time in Vienna, Mendel began experimenting with the **hybridization** of pea plants. He worked with garden peas because he had access to a number of **purebred** varieties. Mendel kept detailed records and precise notes. His experiments lasted for over 7 years and included 34 different varieties of garden peas. Mendel's work marked the beginning of the modern science of genetics.

In 1865, Mendel presented the results of his work to the Society for the Study of Natural Sciences. Unfortunately, the scientific world took little interest in his findings at that time.

Working with Probability

To understand genetics, you need to understand the basic concepts of probability, which is the branch of mathematics that measures the likelihood that a particular event will occur. Probability can be written as a fraction from 0 to 1, as a decimal from 0 to 1, as a percent from 0% to 100%, or as a ratio.

Often, we want to know what our "chances" are before starting an activity. We use numbers from 0 to 1 to indicate the likelihood that an event will occur. The closer this number gets to 0, the "less likely" it is that the event will occur. An event with a probability of 0 is "impossible." The closer the number gets to 1, the more "likely" it is that the event will occur. An event with a probability of 1, or 100%, is "certain." Have you ever asked your mom or dad if you could stay out late on a school night, only to get the reply "not likely"? This means that your chances of being allowed to stay out late are not very good. This is also a form of probability.

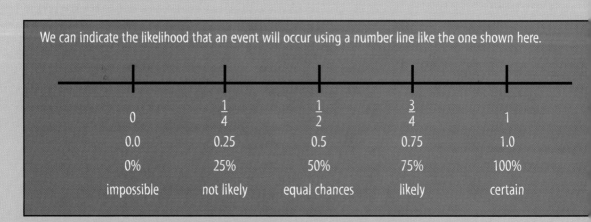

We can indicate the likelihood that an event will occur using a number line like the one shown here.

0	$\frac{1}{4}$	$\frac{1}{2}$	$\frac{3}{4}$	1
0.0	0.25	0.5	0.75	1.0
0%	25%	50%	75%	100%
impossible	not likely	equal chances	likely	certain

Suppose the weatherperson on your local news announces that there is an 80% chance of rain on Tuesday. This means that it is "likely" to rain. It does not mean that it will definitely rain. Just to be safe, you might want to take your umbrella to school on Tuesday. The weatherperson announces that there is only a 10% chance of showers on Wednesday. This means that it is "not likely" that you will need your umbrella. Both of these are predictions based on probability. Neither of the forecasts are "certain."

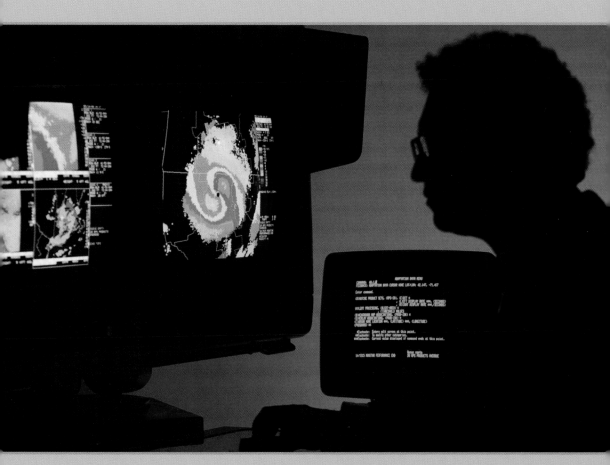

Weather forecasting is just 1 area of life in which probability plays a role. You may encounter probability many times a day. For example, let's say that 2 of your classmates, Maria and José, are running for class president. Since there are only 2 people running for class president, they each have 1 chance out of 2 possible outcomes to win the election. Both candidates have an equal chance of winning the election. The probability of either classmate winning the election can be expressed with the fraction $\frac{1}{2}$, the ratio 1 : 2, the decimal 0.5, or as 50%.

Probability is also a measure of the number of times an event is expected to happen if an experiment is repeated a very large number of times. Let's say you have a bag with 4 colored marbles. The marbles are red, blue, green, and black. If you draw out 1 marble without looking, what are the chances the marble will be red? What are the chances the marble will be purple?

Since there is only 1 red marble out of 4 total marbles, you have a 1-in-4 chance of drawing the red marble. We can show this using a fraction.

$\frac{1}{4}$ ← desired outcome (red marble)

← total number of possible outcomes (4 marbles)

To change this to a percent, we divide 1 by 4, and multiply by 100.

$1 \div 4 = .25$

$0.25 \times 100 = 25\%$ This tells us that, after a large number of trials, we should draw a red marble 25% of the time.

Since there are no purple marbles in the bag, the probability of drawing a purple marble is 0 : 4, or 0%. In other words, it is "impossible" to draw a purple marble.

What is the probability of drawing a purple marble if *all* the marbles in the bag are purple? You would have 4 chances out of 4 possible outcomes to draw a purple marble, which can be expressed with the ratio 4 : 4, or 100%. This means that it is "certain" you will draw a purple marble.

An easy way to experiment with probability is by flipping a coin. Although you cannot tell before the toss whether the result will be heads or tails, you do know that these are the only possible outcomes. It is often helpful to visualize the outcomes of an experiment with a tree diagram. A tree diagram will help you to see all of the possible outcomes of an experiment.

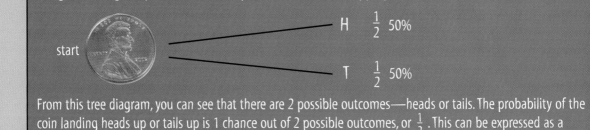

Using a tree diagram, you can see all the possible outcomes of flipping a coin.

start

H $\frac{1}{2}$ 50%

T $\frac{1}{2}$ 50%

From this tree diagram, you can see that there are 2 possible outcomes—heads or tails. The probability of the coin landing heads up or tails up is 1 chance out of 2 possible outcomes, or $\frac{1}{2}$. This can be expressed as a decimal (0.5), a percent (50%), and a ratio (1 : 2).

Now let's say that you are flipping 2 coins. Suppose the first coin lands tails up. Perhaps you are thinking that the second coin has to land heads up since there is a 50% chance of either tails or heads landing face up, and tails has already landed face up. However, this doesn't always happen. Why?

Each toss of a coin is a new event, and the probability starts over. If the first coin lands tails up, the second coin could also land tails up. It could also land heads up. The results of the second event are independent of the results of the first event. The math box on page 11 shows all the possible outcomes for tossing 2 coins.

When tossing 2 coins, we need to extend the tree diagram we made for a single coin.

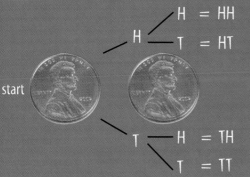

$$H \diagdown \begin{matrix} H & = & HH \\ T & = & HT \end{matrix}$$

start

$$T \diagdown \begin{matrix} H & = & TH \\ T & = & TT \end{matrix}$$

This tree diagram shows that when flipping 2 coins, there are 4 possible outcomes: {HH, HT, TH, TT}.

The set of all possible results of an experiment is known as a sample space.

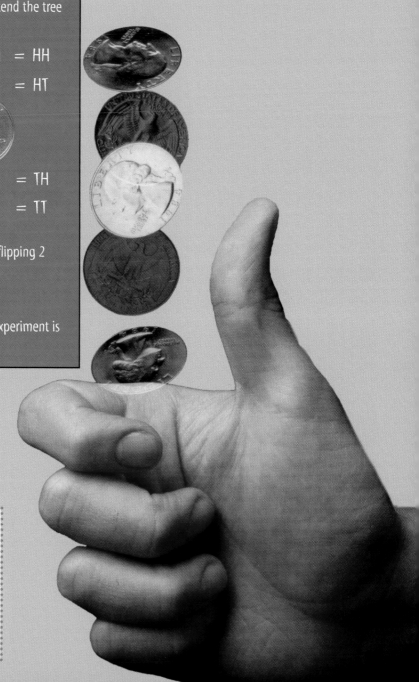

A sample space shows all the possible outcomes of an experiment. The outcomes are written between brackets.

Tree diagrams are helpful in determining the possible outcomes of an experiment. They are also helpful when you need to determine the probability of an event occurring. Let's use the tree diagram we created on page 11 to determine the probability of tossing 2 coins and having both land tails up. Since the probability of the first coin landing tails up is $\frac{1}{2}$, and the probability of the second coin landing tails up is $\frac{1}{2}$, then the probability of both coins landing tails up is $\frac{1}{2}$ x $\frac{1}{2}$, or $\frac{1}{4}$. This tells us that out of 4 possible outcomes—illustrated by the tree diagram and sample space—you have 1 chance out of 4 of tossing 2 tails, or a $\frac{1}{4}$ chance.

Suppose you flipped 1 coin and rolled 1 die. What is the probability of tossing heads up on the coin and rolling the number 5 on the die? Let's use a tree diagram to find out.

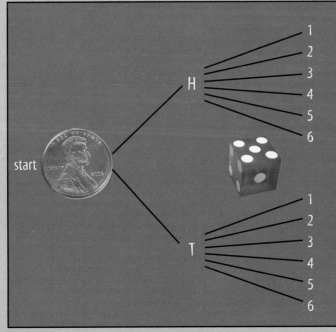

sample space:

{H1, H2, H3, H4, H5, H6, T1, T2, T3, T4, T5, T6}

As we can see from the tree diagram, there is a $\frac{1}{2}$ chance of tossing heads and a $\frac{1}{6}$ chance of rolling a 5. So, $\frac{1}{2}$ x $\frac{1}{6}$ = $\frac{1}{12}$. This means that we have 1 chance out of 12 possible outcomes of tossing heads and rolling a 5.

We can also see this by reading the sample space. Out of the 12 possible outcomes in the sample space, only 1 is H5 (heads and 5). Therefore, the probability of tossing heads and rolling a 5 is $\frac{1}{12}$, or 1 : 12.

The fraction $\frac{1}{12}$ is approximately 0.083. We get this decimal by dividing 1 by 12. To change this into a percent, multiply 0.083 by 100 to get 8.3%. This means that, when conducting the coin-and-die experiment outlined on page 12, only 8.3% of the trials will result in a heads up on the coin and a 5 on the die.

Theoretical and Experimental Probability

The probability of tossing a coin so it lands heads up (or tails up) is 50%. Why is it, then, that when tossing a coin we do not always get heads on 1 flip and tails on the next?

There are 2 types of probability. **Theoretical probability** is the number of times that an event *should* occur if an experiment is repeated an **infinite** number of times. This is what you would predict or expect to happen. We determine theoretical probability by dividing the number of desired outcomes by the number of possible outcomes.

Once you've made a prediction, it is time to conduct the experiment. The results may be different from what you predicted using theoretical probability. **Experimental probability** is what *actually* happens when you run an experiment a number of times. We can determine experimental probability by dividing the number of times the desired outcome actually occurs by the number of trials in the experiment.

$$\text{theoretical probability} = \frac{\text{number of desired outcomes}}{\text{number of possible outcomes}}$$

$$\text{experimental probability} = \frac{\text{number of times the desired outcome actually occurs}}{\text{number of trials in the experiment}}$$

Let's say you have a bag with 4 colored marbles: blue, red, green, and yellow. What are the chances of drawing a red marble?

The theoretical probability of drawing a red marble is $\frac{1}{4}$, or 25%. The number 1 is the number of desired outcomes. The number 4 is the number of possible outcomes.

$1 \div 4 = 0.25$, or 25%

After trying this experiment 100 times, let's say you actually drew a red marble 27 times. So the experimental probability is $\frac{27}{100}$, or 27%.

$27 \div 100 = 0.27$, or 27%

Notice that the experimental probability of 27% is very close to the theoretical probability of 25%.

Let's say that your aunt and uncle are expecting a new baby. There are only 2 possible outcomes: a boy or a girl. If your aunt and uncle want to know the chances of having a boy, the laws of probability can be applied. Out of the 2 possible outcomes, only 1 outcome is a boy. The probability of having a boy would be 1 outcome out of 2 possible outcomes, or 1 out of 2. This means that there is a 50% chance of having a boy. It also means that there is a 50% chance of having a girl.

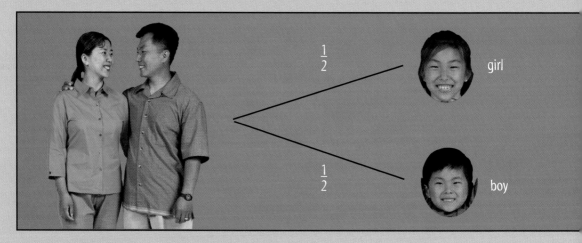

As in the case of tossing coins, each birth is an independent event. Each time a new birth occurs, the probability of having a boy or a girl starts over. This is why some families have all boys or all girls.

The tree diagram below shows that the probability of having 3 boys would be 1 out of 8, or $\frac{1}{8}$. The sample space for this tree diagram shows the same thing. Out of 8 possible outcomes, only 1 is BBB, or 3 boys. Therefore, the probability of having 3 boys is $\frac{1}{8}$, or 1 : 8.

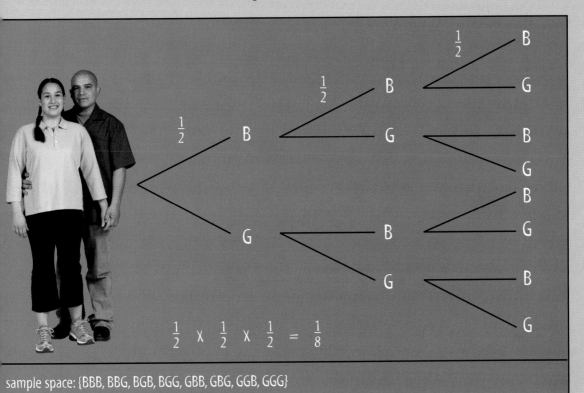

$$\frac{1}{2} \times \frac{1}{2} \times \frac{1}{2} = \frac{1}{8}$$

sample space: {BBB, BBG, BGB, BGG, GBB, GBG, GGB, GGG}

If we simply wanted to find out how many outcomes there would be when having 3 babies, we could use the counting principle. Each time a couple has a baby, there are 2 possible outcomes—a boy or a girl. So, using the counting principle, you can see that the total number of possible outcomes would be 2 x 2 x 2 = 8. This is also what the sample space shows.

Combinations

Sometimes we need to know the total number of combinations that are possible, rather than the likelihood of an event happening. Pretend you are going on a trip, and you need to pack a suitcase. To save room, you decide to pack clothes that you can mix and match to make different combinations. If you bring 2 shirts and 2 pairs of pants, what is the total number of combinations that you will have on your trip? Let's create a tree diagram to help us answer this question.

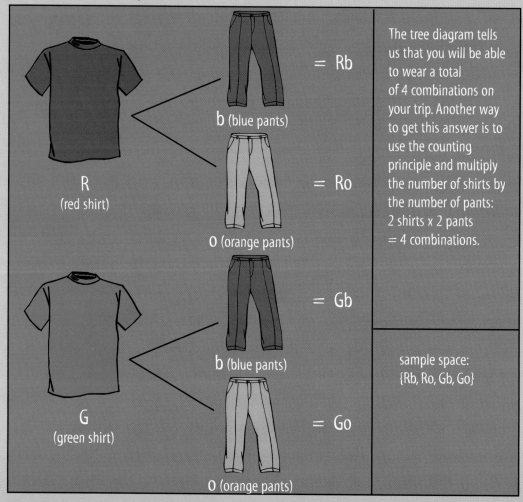

= Rb

b (blue pants)

R
(red shirt)

= Ro

O (orange pants)

= Gb

b (blue pants)

G
(green shirt)

= Go

O (orange pants)

The tree diagram tells us that you will be able to wear a total of 4 combinations on your trip. Another way to get this answer is to use the counting principle and multiply the number of shirts by the number of pants: 2 shirts x 2 pants = 4 combinations.

sample space:
{Rb, Ro, Gb, Go}

We can also use something called a Punnett square to find out how many combinations you can make with the clothes you are bringing on your trip. The Punnett square was devised by an English scientist named Reginald Punnett. In the early 20th century, scientists began to see the value of Gregor Mendel's work. Punnett conducted studies with chickens similar to the work Mendel conducted with pea plants. Punnett devised a simple way to illustrate all the possible **gene** combinations in an offspring based on the pairs of genes inherited from 2 parents. Today we call this method the Punnett square.

First, make a grid like a tic-tac-toe board. Fill in the shirts in the top row, and the pants in the left column. Then find the box where each row and column cross, and fill in that box with the appropriate combination of letters. This Punnett square shows that you can make 4 combinations with 2 shirts and 2 pairs of pants.

red shirt = S
green shirt = s

blue pants = P
orange pants = p

	S	s
P	SP	sP
p	Sp	sp

Genetics and Probability

You have seen how probability applies to tossing coins and to determining the chances of having a boy or girl, but how did Gregor Mendel use probability in determining genetic inheritance? Mendel experimented on thousands of pea plants. During the 7 years that he conducted his experiments, Mendel recorded hundreds of trials and detailed notes on the results. Then he used mathematical probability to analyze his results. Using the principles of probability, Mendel could estimate the likelihood of gene inheritance from 1 generation to the next. Today, the same laws of probability that Mendel used to discover the basic principles of genetic inheritance in pea plants are used to study human genetics.

One of the characteristics that Mendel studied was seed shape. Mendel found that the seeds of some pea plants had a round shape and others had a wrinkled shape. Seed shape in green peas is an inherited feature known as a **character**. The variations of this character, such as round seeds or wrinkled seeds, are known as **traits**. Eye color in humans is an example of a character Brown and blue eye colors are examples of traits.

Eye color isn't the only human character that can be explained through the study of genetic inheritance. Other human characters include hair color and height.

The characters of an individual—such as eye color or seed shape—are determined by inherited factors called genes. Mendel discovered that an individual receives 1 gene from each parent for each character. In Mendel's experiments with garden peas, he found that each parent passed on 1 gene for seed shape that was either **dominant** or **recessive**. Each of these genes is called an **allele**. If an individual receives a dominant allele from 1 parent and a recessive allele from the other parent, the dominant allele masks the appearance of the recessive allele. The allele for brown eyes, for example, is dominant, and often masks the allele for blue eyes, which is recessive. This is why brown eye color is more common than blue eye color.

When you look at a person or a plant, you see many different physical characteristics. The physical characteristics of an organism—such as seed shape or eye color—are known as **phenotypes**. A phenotype is the physical trait that we see when we look at an individual. The pair of genes that create that character is called the **genotype**. A genotype is the combination of alleles that create a physical trait. Mendel represented genotypes in pea plants using pairs of letters. Each letter represents a single allele inherited from each parent. Capital letters stand for dominant genes, and lowercase letters stand for recessive genes.

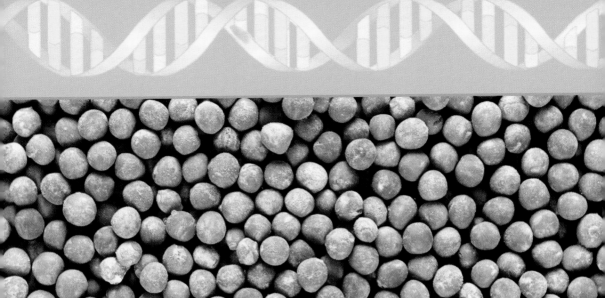

dominant gene for seed shape—round

recessive gene for seed shape—wrinkled

When we see a wrinkled garden pea seed, we are looking at its phenotype for seed shape. We know that the genotype for wrinkled seeds must be 2 recessive alleles, or ss. This is because dominant alleles mask recessive alleles and create a round seed phenotype.

The genotype for each character is made up of 2 alleles, 1 from each parent. Mendel found that it is possible for a genotype to have 2 dominant alleles. Two dominant alleles for seed shape result in round seeds. He represented this with 2 capital letters: SS. It is also possible to have 2 recessive alleles, which results in wrinkled seeds. Mendel represented this with 2 lowercase letters: ss. The condition of having 2 of the same allele—both dominant or both recessive—is called **homozygous**.

However, Mendel discovered that not all genotypes are homozygous. Sometimes an individual receives a dominant allele from 1 parent and a recessive allele from the other parent. When a pea plant has 1 dominant allele and 1 recessive allele (Ss), the dominant allele masks the recessive allele. This results in a round seed shape. The condition of having 1 dominant allele and 1 recessive allele is called **heterozygous**.

genotype	phenotype
SS (homozygous)	round seed shape
Ss (heterozygous)	round seed shape
ss (homozygous)	wrinkled seed shape

A plant that is homozygous for round seed shape has 2 dominant alleles (SS), so the probability of passing on a dominant allele is $\frac{2}{2}$, or 100%. A plant that is homozygous for wrinkled seed shape has 2 recessive alleles (ss). The probability of passing on a recessive allele is $\frac{2}{2}$, or 100%. However, a plant that is heterozygous for seed shape has 1 dominant allele and 1 recessive allele (Ss). The probability of passing on a dominant allele is $\frac{1}{2}$, or 50%. The probability is the same for passing on a recessive allele.

pea plant

Plants that are homozygous are called "purebred plants." Heterozygous offspring of homozygous plants are known as "hybrids."

Mendel began his experiments using purebred pea plants, or pea plants that were homozygous for a given character, in this case seed shape. In the first round of experiments, Mendel bred a pea plant that was homozygous for round seeds (SS) with a pea plant that was homozygous for wrinkled seeds (ss). Since each parent gave a single allele to the offspring and both parents were homozygous, 100% of the offspring were heterozygous for round seed shape (Ss). All of the pea plants had round seeds.

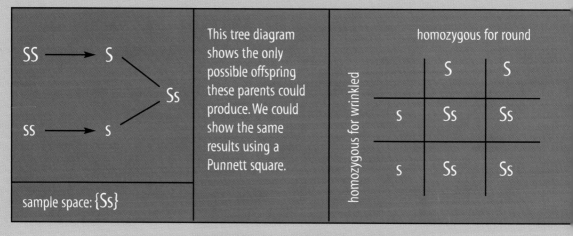

This tree diagram shows the only possible offspring these parents could produce. We could show the same results using a Punnett square.

sample space: {Ss}

Once Mendel was finished with the first round, he bred 2 of the heterozygous plants. What are the chances that 2 heterozygous pea plants could produce an offspring with wrinkled seeds? Let's use what we've learned about probability to find out.

We can see from the Punnett square below that breeding 2 heterozygous plants will result in 3 possible outcomes: {SS, Ss, ss}. The chances of producing a plant that is homozygous for round seeds is $\frac{1}{4}$, or 25%. The chances of producing a plant that is heterozygous for round seeds $\frac{2}{4}$, or 50%. This means 75% of the offspring should have round seeds.

The chances of 2 heterozygous plants producing a plant that is homozygous for wrinkled seeds is $\frac{1}{4}$, or 25%. So, theoretical probability tells us that out of every 4 plants, we should produce 1 plant with wrinkled seeds.

We can use a Punnett square to show all the possible combinations of alleles from 2 heterozygous parent plants.

	S	s
S	SS	Ss
s	Ss	ss

homozygous round seeds (SS)	1 : 4
heterozygous round seeds (Ss)	2 : 4
homozygous wrinkled seeds (ss)	1 : 4

Mendel crossbred thousands of pea plants and observed the traits of each generation. In addition to seed shape, he tracked the development of 6 other traits, including seed color and plant height. His research revealed the basic ideas of modern genetics. Mendel discovered that the inheritance of each trait closely follows the rules of probability. Over a large number of trials, Mendel concluded that pairs of alleles separate randomly when 2 parents produce an offspring. The rules of probability decide which allele each parent will pass on to its child. Today, this idea is known as Mendel's Law of Segregation. Dominant alleles mask recessive alleles. The result of this is that over a long period of time, dominant traits appear 75% of the time, which is times more often than recessive traits.

Mendel also concluded that offspring inherit traits independent of other traits. In other words, offspring do not inherit all dominant traits or all recessive traits. This means that a pea plant could have a wrinkled seed shape, but also exhibit a dominant trait for another character, such as seed color. Seed shape and seed color are 2 independent events, and the probability starts over when considering each character. Today, this idea is known as Mendel's Law of Independent Assortment.

> **Look at the 2 plant types on page 29. Wrinkled seeds and short plant height are both recessive traits. What is the probability of producing a short plant with wrinkled seeds when breeding these 2 parent plants?**

1: SS, TT (homozygous for dominant seed shape and dominant plant height)

2: ss, tt (homozygous for recessive seed shape and recessive plant height)

character is independent of the other. So we to use 2 Punnett squares: 1 to find the total ber of combinations for seed shape and the to find the total number of combinations for height.

	S	S
s	Ss	Ss
s	Ss	Ss

	T	T
t	Tt	Tt
t	Tt	Tt

Punnett squares show that 100% of the ring will be heterozygous for seed shape and height. Since dominant alleles mask recessive s, there is a 0% chance of producing offspring wrinkled seeds and short height. If we used 2 e offspring from the bottom experiment as arents for the next experiment, what is the ability of producing a short offspring? Use a ett square to find out.

The Father of Modern Genetics

Mendel died on January 6, 1884, without knowing that his experiments significantly contributed to modern science and the study of human genetics. In the early 1900s, scientists rediscovered Mendel's work. The genetic investigations and discoveries that Gregor Mendel had made many years before helped to explain the results that scientists were seeing in their own experiments with hybridization. Today the world of science appreciates the significance of Mendel's work and his discovery of the basic principles of genetic inheritance. Gregor Mendel has become known as the father of modern genetics.

Mendel would not have been able to develop his theories without the concepts of probability. Scientists today use probability in many fields of study, from genetics to space exploration. If you dream of being a scientist someday, keep working with math problems that involve probability!

Glossary

allele (uh-LEEL) One of several forms of a gene.

character (KEHR-ihk-tuhr) One of the features—such as eye color—that make up an individual.

dominant (DAH-muh-nuhnt) Prevailing over all others.

experimental probability (ihk-spehr-uh-MEHN-tuhl prah-buh-BIH-luh-tee) The actual results of an experiment.

gene (JEEN) A single unit of hereditary material located in a cell.

genetic (juh-NEH-tik) Related to or controlled by genes.

genotype (JEE-nuh-typ) The genes that make up a trait in an individual.

heterozygous (heh-tuh-roh-ZY-guhs) Having 2 different alleles for a single character, such as seed shape in pea plants (Ss).

homozygous (hoh-moh-ZY-guhs) Having 2 identical alleles for a single character, such as seed shape in pea plants (SS or ss).

hybridization (hy-bruh-duh-ZAY-shun) The act of breeding organisms with different alleles for a single character. The offspring that result are often called hybrids.

infinite (IN-fuh-nuht) Endless.

inheritance (in-HAIR-uh-tuhns) The receiving of genetic information by offspring from parents.

phenotype (FEE-nuh-type) The physical appearance of a trait in an individual.

purebred (PYUR-brehd) Having identical alleles for each character.

recessive (rih-SEH-sihv) Having no phenotypic effect when paired with a dominant allele.

theoretical probability (thee-uh-REH-tih-kuhl prah-buh-BIH-luh-tee) The expected results of an experiment if it were repeated an infinite number of times.

trait (TRAYT) A variation of a character in an organism, such as blue eye color.

Index

A
allele(s), 22, 24, 25, 26, 27, 28, 29

B
Brunn, Austria, 4

C
certain, 6, 7
character(s), 20, 22, 24, 26, 28, 29
combination(s), 18, 19, 22, 27, 29

D
dominant, 22, 23, 24, 25, 28, 29

E
event(s), 8, 10, 12, 14, 16, 18, 28
experiment(s), 8, 10, 12, 14, 15, 20, 22, 26, 29, 30
experimental probability, 14, 15

G
genotype(s), 22, 24

H
Heizendorf, Austria, 4
heterozygous, 24, 25, 26, 27, 29
homozygous, 24, 25, 26, 27, 29
hybridization, 4, 30

I
impossible, 6, 8

L
likely, 6, 7

M
Mendel's Law of Independent Assortment, 28
Mendel's Law of Segregation, 28

N
not likely, 6, 7

O
Olmutz Philosophical Institute, 4
outcome(s), 8, 10, 11, 12, 14, 15, 16, 17, 27

P
phenotype(s), 22
Punnett, Reginald, 19
Punnett square(s), 19, 26, 27, 29
purebred, 4, 26

R
recessive, 22, 23, 24, 25, 28, 29

S
sample space, 11, 12, 17, 18

T
theoretical probability, 14, 15, 27
trait(s), 20, 22, 28
tree diagram(s), 10, 11, 12, 17, 18, 26

U
University of Vienna, 4